D1058742

How to Meditate with Your Dog

An Introduction to Meditation for Dog Lovers

How to Meditate with Your Dog

An Introduction to Meditation for Dog Lovers

James Jacobson
Kristine Chandler Madera

MAUI
MEDIA

Published by:
Maui Media, LLC.
www.MauiMedia.com

Library of Congress Control Number: 2005931554

How To Meditate With Your Dog: An Introduction To
Meditation For Dog Lovers / James Jacobson with Kristine
Chandler Madera.

ISBN 0-975-26311-0 Hardcover

Cover and Text Design by Bob Stovern
Cover Photograph by Steve Brinkman
Back Cover Photographs by Lori A. Cheung, thePetPhotographer.com

We would like to thank the following agencies and individuals
for permission to reprint the following:

Dog photographs printed by permission of Lori A. Cheung,
whose dog portraits illuminate the canine soul, and capture
the magic and inner sparkle of each dog. Thanks also to the
dogs: Fresco Bloomberg, Muddy Waters, Flash, Winona
Louise Gordon.

Andertoons. Reprinted by permission of Mark Anderson.

>> Continued on Page 174

"A dog wags its tail with its heart."

~ Martin Buxbaum, Author

Table of Contents

 # Foreword

In Tibet, it is believed that some dogs are inhabited by the souls of Dalai Lamas as they depart their earthly bodies on the way to Nirvana.

In Greek mythology, dogs were the protectors and companions of gods. They have also been part of creation stories. Across traditions, dogs have been at the center of human spiritual life.

I was born into a family of dog lovers. My fondest childhood memories are of the loving and playful companionship of Brownie and Blackie, our two Springer Spaniels. I always knew they were my best friends and the finest of God's creation, but until reading this book, it had not occurred to me what fine teachers of meditation dogs can be.

How To Meditate With Your Dog: An Introduction To Meditation For Dog Lovers brings the love that we have for our dogs into the center of a meditative practice.

Meditation can be a daunting prospect. Oftentimes people don't believe that they have the time or the "quiet of mind" to practice meditation.

Meditating with a dog is multitasking in a beautiful and sensible way. As we meditate, we improve our well-being while bonding with our dogs. We dog lovers can always find time to spend with our pooches.

In a dog, we have a natural, non-dogmatic, focal point for meditation. It is the spiritual connection with another being, who also happens to be our personal canine meditation guru.

Meditation has been part of spiritual and religious tradition for almost as long as dogs have been our companions. It's a natural extension to sharing life with a dog.

In fact, after reading this book, I'm inclined to wonder if it was dogs that taught us to meditate in the first place.

~ Reverend Mary Omwake
    Co-founder, Gandhi & King Season for Peace & Nonviolence

12-30

 # Introduction

Meditation has been a lifelong practice for me.

As a boy I would sit and quiet my mind as a way to relax. It wasn't until later that I understood that my increased ability to focus, to look at almost any situation objectively, and to enjoy the present moment (most of the time anyway) stemmed from this daily practice.

Over the years, I've seen meditation transform lives—both canine and human.

Excitable dogs become calmer. Aggressive dogs become more loving. Dogs that are already easygoing become an even more peaceful presence in their caretakers' lives.

For humans, science has proven that just a few minutes of meditation aids in relaxation and stress relief. That alone is a powerful benefit in our fast-paced society. But there is so much more to be had.

Meditation helps us become more objective, and, as a result, more compassionate. This enables us to find contentment and acceptance of the circumstances in our lives. Simultaneously, a meditation practice helps us cultivate intuition and improve the ability to focus. Those skills are immeasurably important in both setting and achieving personal goals.

One of the sweetest gifts is that meditation shows us how to savor the present moment—the only moment we have.

Meditation helps me stay calm in times of great stress, and I would argue that it has helped my dog, Maui, too.

A few weeks after moving into our new house, Maui lost her vision. She was ten years old, but still the blindness was sudden and unexpected. It came on literally overnight.

It was total darkness for a dog who, only a day earlier, lounged on the porch peering out over all the new trees and bushes to explore in her new home.

My beloved dog was thrust in a world of darkness. With her head to the ground, she took one tentative half step after another, hoping, it seemed, to sniff out a familiar spot that might turn the lights back on. Instead she bumped into a wall. With each successive attempt, she whimpered louder as she got more confused. I was heartsick—here we were in this unfamiliar, multilevel house and she couldn't see, or even smell, her way around.

I took her to the vet who performed tests and diagnosed her with a relatively rare canine ailment known as Sudden Acquired Retinal Degeneration Syndrome. SARDS, as it is known in the veterinary community, is a condition where the retina is rejected by the body and breaks apart—sometimes overnight. There is no cure.

The second I heard the prognosis, a wave of panic washed over me. The shock lasted for a moment or two. But then I caught myself. I took a few deep breaths and went into my meditation mode. I took a deep breath, and then mentally stepped away from the panic and focused on Maui. Panic, I knew, wouldn't help, and just knowing that enabled me to let it go.

More relaxed, I accepted the situation, and even became content with it. To fight it would do no good. That didn't mean, though, that I gave up and did nothing.

Maui and I had meditated together for most of her ten years, and it seemed to me that expanding the practice was the best thing that we could do. I went home from the vet, perched Maui on my lap, and closed my eyes. We sat in dark stillness and meditated together for nearly an hour.

After the hour, both Maui and I were calmer. Although she still couldn't see, she didn't seem as anxious—she no longer whimpered while trying to find her way around. I gave her a treat, which she could smell but couldn't get at until I put it directly in front of her mouth.

I went downstairs to my laptop and started my Internet research about SARDS. I joined an online support group for people with blind dogs and learned tricks such as using particular perfumes to mark various areas in the house. I was accepting that this was a challenge that both Maui and I could overcome. You could, I reckoned, teach an old dog new tricks.

As I sat on the floor in my furniture-less home (the furniture had yet to arrive), I wondered how Maui might navigate the new surroundings with the familiar smells of the old furniture. Deep inside, I knew that things would turn out all right, but part of me was still skeptical.

Hours passed as I clattered away on my laptop, seeking to learn everything I could about how best to adapt. I would occasionally look up at Maui who was curled up in a ball resting no more than a few feet away. She wasn't asleep; her eyes were half-open, her gaze unfocused. She was in a natural dog meditation state I call hound-lounge.

I will never know what, or even if, she was thinking during the hours she spent in that deep, comfortable, restorative hound-lounge. What I do know is that at the stroke of five o'clock, something magical happened.

The doorbell rang.

Maui jumped from her hound-lounge, spun around once, raced out of the room, down the hall, bounded up the steps and to the front door— barking all the way. She was adroit and sure-foot-ed. I opened the door to greet two neighborhood children and Maui stood on her hind legs and sniffed their hands for possible treats.

To my amazement, and against all the wis-dom of veterinary medicine, my dog could see! Her eyesight had returned.

During the next few months her vision would wax and wane, punctuated by several daylong episodes of complete blindness. Throughout it, we meditated together, and Maui hound-lounged by herself. With medita-tion, and a modest dose of steroid drugs, Maui licked her blindness. Vets are puzzled by it, and sing the praises of the medication. I think there was something else at play.

Was it a meditation miracle? I like to think so. But even if it wasn't, I credit my meditation practice with giving me the ability to accept the situation and remain calm enough to help rather than being paralyzed by anger and grief.

There is no downside to meditation. The time that we devote to it, we make up for exponentially in the clarity and peace that it brings to the rest of our day.

Meditating with a dog is particularly time-effective. It's good for us and it's good for our dogs. We both reap the benefits of meditation as we bond on a soul level.

Meditation is a fascinating adventure. Through this book, I invite you and your dog to come along and explore it.

~ James Jacobson

Meditating with Your Dog

"In order to really enjoy a dog, one doesn't merely try to train him to be semi-human. The point of it is to open oneself to becoming partly a dog."

~ Edward Hoagland, Novelist, Essayist

Meditating with Your Dog

"In order to really enjoy a dog, one doesn't merely try to train him to be semi-human. The point of it is to open oneself to becoming partly a dog."

~ Edward Hoagland, Novelist, Essayist

CHAPTER 1

Why Meditate with Your Dog?

Dog lovers are a breed apart.

I know dog lovers who bake homemade dog biscuits, who fill a special stocking at Christmas, and who would forgo a free vacation if they couldn't take their dog.

We dog lovers would try almost anything — if we thought it would be good for our dogs.

But meditating with a dog?

Absolutely.

Meditating with our dogs is one of the most caring things we can do for them. It's a terrific way to bond, and it's good for their health and well-being.

3

Doggy tags jingled as Maui, my eight-pound, white fluff ball of a Maltese traipsed into the room. She spied me sitting on the sofa, took a running jump, and landed in my lap—which is where, given her druthers, she would spend most of her time.

"Hey Maui," I said, scratching behind her ears, which she loves.

She leaned into my fingers for a little deep-tissue scratch. When I stopped, her big brown eyes welled up with contentment as she looked at me. Then she turned a circle or two on my lap and lay down.

I smiled as I watched her breathing slow and her eyes droop to half-open. She was slipping into what I call hound-lounge—that place between wide-eyed wakefulness and a sound doggy-doze where our pooches spend much of their time. Hound-lounge is, I believe, the canine counterpart to human meditation.

Most dogs take quickly to meditating with us. It's natural for them. Dogs are pack animals. They love to cuddle up and hound-lounge with the pack. In fact, this connection is pivotal to a dog's health and happiness.

When I adopted Maui, I became part of her pack. More than that, I became her pack leader.

As pack leader, Maui's contentment is my responsibility. The time we spend meditating together demonstrates to Maui that I love her and that I value the time I spend with her. Meditation creates a peaceful synergy that helps keep our pack life smooth.

But dogs are also keen sensors. They know when we're distracted or upset. Moreover, they reflect our moods back to us. If we are on edge, then so are our dogs.

Meditation helps us pack leaders relax. A peaceful pack leader tends to have a calmer, more amiable dog.

When we take the time to meditate with our dogs, amazing things happen. I've seen dogs that were fearful become braver and more loving; anxious dogs that became zen-ishly calm; dogs that whined and howled for attention become quieter and more content.

I believe this is because when we meditate with our dogs, we connect and communicate love on a deeper level than we do by playing together or hanging out.

The time we spend in meditation is good for our dogs, and it's a great way to bond — but there's more.

Meditation is good for pack leaders, too.

In the first minutes of meditation, stress begins to abate — we feel more serene, our minds clear, and we begin to relax. Those who begin to meditate regularly have even more benefits to look forward to: improved focus, a sense of contentment, better intuition, just to name a few. I describe an in-depth list of benefits in the eighth chapter, Treats For Pack Leaders.

Are you ready to start?

If you are, that's great. If you're hesitant, that's okay, too.

A little caution is as healthy as a nice long stretch after a dognap. Skepticism keeps us limber and helps us to ease into an activity with forethought rather than bounding with all four paws into what might turn out to be a pretty deep mud-puddle.

The main reason I've found people are uncertain about meditation is that it's so subjective.

Simply defined, meditation is the non-judgmental observation of the present moment.

No book or teacher can construct the meditation experience for you. Each person's experience is unique because meditation is about *being*, not *doing*.

Meditation has few, if any, hard and fast rules—and that aspect runs counter to some of the ingrained notions of Western society: hard work, logical progression, achievable goals.

But even Western society has embraced aspects of *being*.

Playing catch with a dog is all about *being*. Sports like baseball, football, or tennis, are perfectly fine, but they are *doing* types of sports—with the achievable goal of winning, with rules and replicable structures for achieving that goal.

**"My therapy is quite simple: I wag my tail and lick
your face until you feel good about yourself again."**

Playing catch with a dog has structure, too: you throw, your dog catches (part of the time anyway), and somehow the ball or the stick or whatever you threw gets back in your hand for you to throw again.

There's no winning or losing, and no real rules. The point is to have fun, to get exercise, and to bond with your dog. There's also that part when the throwing and the catching all work seamlessly, without effort, a sort of zone where we are a dog's hair away from bliss.

Maui's head popped up from my lap. She gazed at me first with a questioning look, then a *knowing* look. Maui is spooky like that sometimes—racing to the refrigerator the moment I think of food, tail wagging by the door just as I get in the mood for a walk.

This time, she jumped off my lap and nudged at the little plastic flying mini-disc, which I call a bliss-disc, that poked out from under the couch.

She was after a game of catch.

I picked up the bliss-disc and threw it at a barstool leg.

"Go get it girl," I called after Maui as she ran toward the stool and then tried to jump for the disc as it bounced off the barstool leg.

She dragged the bliss-disc back to me for another go. I aimed at the planter this time, which it hit with a soft thud. Maui never seems to mind where I throw the disc, or whether or not she catches it.

She has no use for the *doing* of the Western mind. But then, why would she? Doggy mind is so much more fun: lots of play, abundant spontaneous expression, the inherent joy in a present-moment state-of-being—all of which are also fruits of meditation.

Playing catch with the bliss-disc isn't about achieving, it's about experiencing; it's not about *doing*, it's about *being*. It's one of those proverbial win-win situations—just like meditation.

Maui snatched up the bliss-disc and scampered back to me, then dropped the disc at my feet and yapped in excitement. I could tell I was in for a long game of bliss-disc.

But that's okay; playing with Maui is an exercise in *being*. My life, like most people's, proliferates with *doing*—running a business, staying in shape, tinkering Mr. Fix-it style around the house.

Meditation, too, helps bring a little more *being* into our lives.

Still skeptical?

You may share my mother's concern—that if friends and neighbors saw me meditating with Maui, they'd think I'd lost my mind.

That might be true. But the people who think that meditating with a dog is crazy are probably the same ones who specify that their leftover restaurant food should be placed in a "people" bag rather than a "doggy" bag.

It seems to me that dog lovers would find the idea of meditating with their dogs as perfectly natural. In fact, most dog lovers *already* meditate with their pooches—they just don't call it that.

It happens when we stretch out on the floor with our dogs or maybe curl up on the couch. The world around us turns quiet and we zone out. In the stillness, the line between the dog and us blurs, almost as if we have become one.

In this state, our thoughts slow down. For a moment or two at a time, it seems that we're not thinking at all.

I call these moments "spontaneous meditation." They give a glimpse of the peace, the feeling of connection, and the bliss that we can gain from intentional meditation.

Meditation is simple.

Anyone can meditate. All you need is the belief that you can do it—then to sit down and start.

Any dog can meditate, too.

Maui was still a puppy when we began meditating together more than a decade ago. She was a natural meditator—most dogs are. So it wasn't long before she became my meditation guru.

Over the years, I've shared the magic of meditating with Maui with friends, with other dog lovers, even with skeptics. Some of these people had dogs that they considered hyper, intractable, the antithesis of meditative.

You know what?

Every one of those dogs had a meditation guru inside just panting to be released.

If you have a dog, then you have a guru, too.

"Isn't that true, Maui?" I said as she walked up to me with the bliss-disc hanging from her mouth.

She looked dog-tired. She'd chased the disc and brought it back at least twenty times. I tossed it again, but she didn't run after it. She just gazed up at me and her big brown eyes told me all I needed to know.

I sat on the floor and lifted her onto my lap. She closed her eyes and gave a sigh.

"Is that what you're after?" I said, rubbing her neck.

But she was already well into hound-lounge, and I knew that she was too relaxed to respond to every little stimuli. About the only things that will bring Maui out of her hound-lounge before she is ready are the doorbell ringing or opening the refrigerator door.

Dogs are natural meditators.

If we watch our dogs and absorb some of their innate dog nature, we can become meditators, too.

Just the Bones

Why Meditate with Your Dog?

- It promotes health, happiness and relaxation for both dogs and humans.

- It is a terrific way to bond with your dog.

- It expresses your love to your dog.

- It helps you appreciate *being* rather than *doing*.

"Dogs are the most amazing creatures...
for me they are the role model for being alive."

– Gilda Radner, Comedienne

CHAPTER 2

The Bare Bones

Meditation is simple, but how exactly do we meditate with a dog?

What are the "bare bones," so to speak?

This is what Maui and I do.

Most days Maui finds it fun to bark endlessly a few minutes before my alarm goes off. I think she believes this is a contribution to our meditation process.

In any case, I get up, turn off the alarm, take a shower, put on my favorite Turkish cotton bathrobe, and then whistle through the house as I make my way to the room where we meditate.

"How can we attain serenity with him
bouncing a ball off my head?"

Marmaduke: © United Feature Syndicate, Inc.

When I start whistling, Maui comes running. She usually bounds past me into the room and waits, panting, as I sit in our meditation chair. Then she jumps onto my lap and, usually, lies down.

If I want music, I turn on my favorite meditation CD.

I rest my hands on Maui, usually with one hand on her chest and the other on her back. This contact helps to strengthen our bond during meditation.

Once these preliminaries are done, we settle into the essence of our meditation.

I close my eyes, and focus on Maui's breath. Without conscious effort, my breath and Maui's synchronize. I focus on the synch of our breathing, and it helps take me deeper into the meditation.

Perfect, right?

Well, about this time, a thought will drift through my mind—what I want for breakfast, what I need to get done for the day, a fragment of a dream I had during the night.

Thoughts are inevitable. Even seasoned meditators have thoughts while meditating. I would bet that the Dalai Lama has thoughts while he meditates. His thoughts may be more profound than mine, but they are still thoughts.

As soon as I observe that I am having a thought, I let it go—gently, without judging the thought or berating myself for having a thought while I am trying to meditate. This process of letting thoughts go is similar across most meditation traditions.

With the thought released, I return my focus to the synch of Maui's breath and mine. Or, if the thought caused me to fall out of synch, I focus on Maui's breath until our breaths synchronize again.

Then another thought comes—it's as predictable as Maui's sudden salivation at the whiff of a t-bone on the grill.

I let go of the new thought, and refocus on the synch of our breaths once again.

I'll let you in on a trick of the meditation trade.

A meditation master once said that if all we do during meditation is to repeat this cycle: observe thoughts, release them, and refocus — then we are meditating.

I meditate for as long as it feels right, observing my thoughts, releasing them, and synchronizing my breath with Maui's.

Then I return slowly to the feeling of my body, to the reality of the room, and to the hound-lounging Maui on my lap.

When I open my eyes, I invariably feel lighter than I did when I started, as if gravity has lost some of its hold.

Colors appear more vivid, objects seem brighter, and my peripheral vision is enhanced. It lasts only a short while, but I'm sure that if a scientist hooked me up to a device that could measure the light sensitivity of my eyes, it would show a marked difference between the time before I began to meditate, and after.

Now, I'm no sage; I'm an ordinary person. And while I think that Maui is an amazing guru of a dog, I make no claim that she is a descendant of a long line of doggy meditation masters. But if together we can find this much peace and this much power during daily meditation, then I'd bet a box of liver snacks that you and your dog can, too.

Just the Bones

The Bare Bones

Here is an example of the steps that I take in my meditation practice with Maui. The following chapters will help you and your dog develop your own meditation rituals.

- We go to our meditation room and sit.

- I may turn on music.

- I place my hands on Maui.

- I close my eyes and focus on Maui's breath.

- Our breathing synchronizes.

- When a thought comes, I let it go and refocus on our breath.

- I continue this process for as long as it feels right.

"The bond with a true dog is as lasting as the ties of this earth can ever be."

~ Konrad Lorenz, Zoologist & Ethnologist

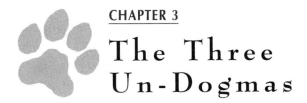

CHAPTER 3
The Three Un-Dogmas

Meditation, in some form, is practiced in most major religions. But since this book is non-dogmatic, we will look at the three un-dogmas that turn spontaneous meditation into deliberate meditation.

The three un-dogmas are: intention, belief, and synergy.

Maui looked up from her spot on the center of the floor, where I would have to step over her in order to go just about anywhere. Her ears twitched as if she caught the scent of something interesting. But then she just yawned, shook her head, and slipped back into hound-lounge.

Maui doesn't need to study about meditation. It's part of dog nature.

INTENTION

Dogs are masters of intention.

Maui stretched, shook her head, and sniffed the air. Then she stood up, bouncy and ready for action. She trotted over to where I sat and narrowed her brown eyes at the couch as if it were part of a conspiracy to hide her bliss-disc — which it was. I hide the disc under there to save my throwing arm.

I scratched behind her ears. "What are you after, girl?"

Maui looked at me, then at the couch. She turned her head to the side and poked her little nose in the slim space between the floor and the couch.

She caught the scent. She knew it was there. She reached out a paw and clawed at the disc.

"Maui, stop," I said, trying to distract her. "Here, girl, want a treat?"

I pulled a liver snack from the snack jar I keep on the counter, waved it in the air while holding my breath because, to be perfectly honest, the liver snack didn't smell all that appealing to my human nose.

Maui ignored me, and reached her paw further under the couch.

I tossed her the treat. She gulped it up and went right back to mining under the couch for her bliss-disc, growling this time.

I'd lost and I knew it.

"All right, girl," I said. I slid a magazine under the couch, behind the disc, and pushed the disc out.

Maui yelped in excitement. I threw the disc across the room, and it smacked into her water bowl.

Oh well, Maui was happy. She'd gotten the object of her intention.

Intention is willful purpose. It is what makes Maui relentless in getting her bliss-disc—or her liver snacks, or whatever her heart desires.

When we sit with the intention to meditate —
when we make meditation our *conscious choice* — we
focus all of our energy toward this end.

Take for example the force of the summer
sun. We can feel its heat against our skin.

Focused energy is more powerful still. That
same sunlight focused through a magnifying
glass can burn a name into a piece of wood.

Similarly, when we focus energy through
intention, we magnify the effect of meditation.

BELIEF

Maui has taught me more about the power of
belief than I could ever have learned on my own.

Maui is usually the smallest adult dog at the
local dog park. But she doesn't act it.

At first, I thought it was because she didn't
know she was small, that somehow this fact
escaped her awareness.

I've come to realize that she does know that
she's shorter than the rest of the dogs. She just

doesn't believe it. More accurately, she doesn't let her diminutive size influence her belief that she is the biggest, bossiest, most alpha-esque dog in the park—anyone with a Chihuahua can attest to that.

She dominates Labradors and Poodles alike. It's not, I'm convinced, that these other dogs have no conception of the size difference. It's because Maui believes in her ability so strongly that it causes the other dogs to believe it, too.

The power of belief can transform us—or it can be our biggest obstacle in achieving our goals.

Sure, we can set intention, but if we don't believe that we can achieve the object of that intention, we never will.

I subscribe to the "fake it 'til you make it" school of belief—it's immediate and it works.

Even if we are not bursting with the belief that we can meditate right away, we can take a lesson from Maui, and act as if we are. We make "I believe" a goal in progress. Don't settle on "I sort of believe," or "I want to believe."

Try this little experiment. Say the words "I *think* I can," and notice how you feel. Then take a breath, and say, "I *know* I can."

Feel the difference?

This sense of *knowing* that we can meditate is one that we cultivate as we continue our practice.

Each time we sit, we set our intention to meditate. We then tell ourselves that we believe we can do it. Over time, that belief becomes real.

SYNERGY

Humans and dogs are symbiotic. We've relied on dogs for over 14,000 years as hunting partners, security guards, and friends. Dogs, too, have relied on us as protectors, providers of food, and as companions. Our lives would be immeasurably less if we, as species, were without each other.

We are so connected that when we sit together in meditation something happens called physiological synchrony. Physiological synchrony is a term coined by researchers to reference the interconnection between emotions and body responses. When we connect with another being, our nervous systems begin to mimic one another. As we meditate with our dogs, our two breathing patterns come into synch, both our heartbeats slow, our nervous systems come into rhythm.

This happens each time Maui and I meditate, and it happens without conscious effort.

This process forms the basis of what we call synergy.

Synergy in meditation is sparked when two or more entities come together united in a single intention, sharing their combined belief.

Whether the intention is prayer, raising money for an animal shelter, or challenging political policy, the effect of two or more entities gathered together is greater than their efforts individually.

I've meditated with people all over the world, with like-minded friends, with famous gurus, even with a group on Capitol Hill.

In each case, I found that the energy of meditating in a group was exponentially more powerful than when I meditated alone. Meditating in a group magnifies the sense of connection, not only to one another, but also to the collective energy of the universe.

Maui ran to me, dropped the bliss-disc at my feet, and cocked her head to the side. Her ears poked out in question, as if she could sniff my hesitation in the use of "collective energy of the universe."

"I'm not sure how else to describe it, Maui," I said. "Everyone has a different name for the creative force—God, Collective Consciousness, Higher Power, The Universe. I'm trying to be diplomatic."

Maui wagged her tail, and then yapped at the bliss-disc. I tossed it for her again—toward a chair. But that didn't seem to matter to her. She chased it anyway.

Because synergy is so powerful, I've always preferred to meditate with a group.

However, groups are difficult to schedule. Unless I was visiting a contemplative community or at a retreat, getting a group together to meditate daily was so challenging that I resigned myself to having to meditate alone.

Then, I had an insight.

I joked to a friend that since dogs are natural meditators, they would make the best meditation partners.

She laughed.

But I knew it was true. Dogs embody non-judgment and unconditional love—traits many people think of when they envision a spiritually attuned being.

Dogs have few, if any, scheduling conflicts. They enjoy being with us, and are almost always willing participants.

I realized then that I didn't need to meditate alone after all—I had Maui.

In the years since, meditation has become a daily ritual for Maui and me. If for some reason I forget to meditate, Maui ambles into our meditation room and sits on my chair to remind me.

In that way, and many others, Maui has become my personal meditation guru.

If you have a dog, then you have a meditation guru, too.

To unleash it, all you need is to set your intention, believe, connect with your dog, and ask her to teach you.

Just the Bones

The Three Un-dogmas

To turn spontaneous meditation into deliberate meditation, use the three undogmas:

- **Intention** is the willful purpose or conscious choice that we bring to an action or state.

- **Belief** is the practice of knowing something to be true.

- **Synergy** in meditation is the law of "where two or more are gathered," meaning that when two or more entities are united in intention and belief, their efforts are exponentially more powerful than their individual efforts.

"All knowledge, the totality of all questions and all answers is contained in the dog."

~ Franz Kafka, Philosopher

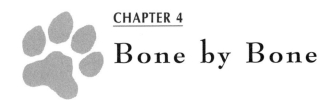

CHAPTER 4

Bone by Bone

Now that you know the basics of my meditation routine:

Do you want to try it?

We'll take it slow, step-by-step, bone-by-bone.

I changed into the robe I use for my meditation, and whistled for Maui as I walked through the house.

Maui came running, but then stopped and looked at me strangely, wondering, I'm sure, what I was doing in my meditation robe at three in the afternoon.

"We're going to meditate, Maui," I said. "And we're going to meditate now."

She gazed at me, still uncertain—much like your dog might look at you the first time you announce, "We're going to meditate."

But in order to meditate, we must first:

DECIDE TO DO IT

Once we choose to meditate, we need to follow through and do it. This is one way that we demonstrate intention.

"I'm serious, Maui," I said. "Come on, we're going to meditate."

Maui tilted her head to one side, her eyes squeezed together, a little leery.

I didn't think Maui wanted to avoid meditation. Normally, she liked it. But I was breaking with routine—we had already meditated this morning.

Maui would join in once she knew what was going on, but right then she was a little confused, as your dog might be the first few times you get ready to meditate.

That's okay; a new routine can be as challenging for our dogs as it is for us—more so actually, as we are the ones who set the routine.

"Come on, girl," I said, pointing toward the meditation room.

Maui still hesitated, but that gave me the chance to go on to the next step.

SET THE STAGE

I walked into the meditation room and turned on the CD that I often meditate to in the mornings.

Having music, especially at first, can help cue our dogs that it is meditation time. Although all we really *need* in order to meditate is a quiet place to sit.

On that note, we want to choose a time when the house around us is quiet—when no one will bother us, with the phone unplugged or at least turned off, no stereos blaring nearby, that sort of thing.

Setting the stage also means readying ourselves for meditation.

I admit that I, too, was a little unsettled meditating at a different time of day than usual. Maui was probably picking up on that. Dogs are great at reflecting emotions.

I closed my eyes and took several long, deep breaths. I began to relax, and then to believe that I could meditate at a time of day when I am usually absorbed in work.

As I relaxed, Maui seemed less unsure and even walked into the meditation room to see what I was doing.

Dogs are also naturally curious, and that can be an advantage when we go on to step three.

GET YOUR DOG

For me this was easy. Maui was slowly grasping what I expected and so walking over to her and picking her up was not a problem. Even when we first started meditating and Maui wasn't used to our routine, she was just eight pounds, so picking her up was rarely difficult—an aerobic activity at times, but not a problem.

If you have more than one dog, I suggest you meditate first with the dog with which you have the greatest rapport.

If your dog is too big to pick up, then you'll need to use another method. Visualization helps. Create an image in your head of your dog doing exactly what you want him to do — dogs are good at reading our mental pictures, though they don't always choose to cooperate.

If the mental image doesn't work, play pack leader. As alpha, it is your privilege to assert your will — take hold of the dog's collar and lead him to the place you want to meditate.

I carried Maui into the meditation room, sat on the chair, and put her on my lap. She gazed up at me as full understanding dawned. She licked my face, then lay down and wiggled her way into a semblance of hound-lounge.

Large dogs are more of a challenge — it's hard to stay in a meditative state with a hundred-fifty pound Great Dane on your lap.

With larger dogs, or dogs that are not allowed on the furniture, lead the dog to the place where you've decided you want to meditate—a particular corner, a special dog bed, wherever it is that you've determined.

Then have the dog sit, and, if possible, lie down. You can sit behind him and stretch your legs out on either side of the dog, or even have your legs loosely encircling him. If this doesn't work, or isn't comfortable for either you or the dog, then have him lie down next to you.

I rest my hands gently on Maui's chest and back because this is generally the most comfortable position. It doesn't matter that you touch your dog with both hands, or really that you touch your dog at all. But the physical contact of our hands on our dogs is reassuring to them. It helps increase the sense of connection between us, and it spurs the process of physiological synchrony.

Remember, too, that your experience may be different than the one I explain here. Meditating with your dog will be as unique as your relationship with your dog.

Being comfortable as we meditate is important. If we need to shift our hands or bodies, or change positions during meditation to stay comfortable, we should, but we should do so mindfully. Reflexive, unconscious movement detracts from meditation.

All right so far? Then we close our eyes, and:

RETURN TO INTENTION

Depending on how long it takes us to go through the previous steps, intention might have flagged. We then restate that we intend to meditate, not just to ourselves, but also, silently, to our dogs.

I turned my attention to Maui's breath, which is a prelude to getting into:

SYNCH

Maui's back rose and fell with her breath. My hands rose and fell with her. I kept my attention on Maui's breath — I could feel it swirl through her body. In a few minutes, without conscious effort, my breathing synchronized with hers.

It may not happen the first time you meditate with your dog, or even the first few times, but eventually, once you and your dog are both comfortable in your meditation ritual, you should be able to ease into this synch.

Maui's breath slowed, and so did mine. I could no longer tell quite where my hands ended and Maui's body began. It felt as if we melted into a force beyond our physical bodies. In our combined meditation, we had created synergy.

Maui and I breathed together in deep synch. I knew we had several minutes of meditation ahead of us, so I shifted a bit to get comfortable.

For me, it's right about this time that the first errant thought floats through my head and I start what I call:

THE CYCLE

Maui lay on my lap, her only movement the expansion and contraction of her lungs as she breathed. She's never given me any indication that she is plagued by a scattered mind when we meditate.

I opened an eye and gazed at Maui's face. She looked perfectly serene.

Dogs make it look so easy.

I closed my eye again, and soon noticed my mind wandering:

How could I possibly describe the cycle in a few sentences? It is such a core part of meditation and I don't want to short change—

Uh oh, I was thinking.

Once I become aware that I'm thinking, a more detached part of me that I call the observer takes over.

The observer is not like a dogcatcher; it doesn't snatch up our thought in a net and fling it into the back of a truck to whisk it away.

The observer is the silent witness to our thoughts. It softly announces, "We are having a thought." Then it recedes without judgment, leaving us with the awareness that we are thinking, and the choice of what we are going to do with our thoughts.

*"It's always 'Sit,' 'Stay,' 'Heel'—never
'Think,' 'Innovate,' 'Be yourself.'"*

The more interesting the thought, the greater the temptation to explore it and see where it goes. But when we let thoughts lead us, we are practicing thinking, not meditation.

So we acknowledge that we had a thought, and gently let it go. There is no crime in thinking; thinking is central to the human experience.

I said to my mind, "Thank you for the thought. I now let it go."

I returned my attention to synch—to the uniting of Maui's breath with mine.

She was breathing a little slower than I was—the anxiety of thinking about the cycle had upped my respiration. I concentrated on Maui's breath and eventually we came back into synch.

But the cycle is such a central experience. Am I explaining it right? I mean—

"We are having a thought," the observer said.

"Okay," I said to my mind. "Thank you for the thought. I now let it go."

I took a deep breath and returned to synch.

Did I remember to turn off the telephone?

"We are having a thought," the observer said.

And so the cycle goes.

The cycle itself has benefits. The process of letting go helps us relax, relieve stress, and practice living in the present moment. Invoking the observer cultivates objectivity. Releasing our thoughts without judgment develops compassion. Coming back to synch every time we let go of a thought aids focus.

But the full spectrum of meditation benefits comes from a place referred to by authors such as Deepak Chopra and Wayne Dyer as:

THE GAP

Maui shifted.

I opened an eye to see if she might be awake and alert again.

But she was just getting comfortable. She looked like she was still in the gap—the space between thoughts.

Maui, like most dogs, spends a lot of time in the gap. When Maui enters hound-lounge, she generally stays in that state until I signal that meditation time is over, or until she hears the front door opening, or smells bacon cooking. Then her intention quickly shifts from meditation to visitors or food or whatever, and off she goes. But while she is on my lap in the meditation chair, I believe that she stays in the gap.

Humans aren't so lucky. Being natural thinkers, we have the habit of filling our minds with thought after thought after thought.

The gap is the silent space between thoughts, an inner stillness that we experience when our minds are quiet.

In meditation, we release our thoughts as they come. So that instead of crowding our minds with things to think about, we try to create space without thoughts so that we can experience the gap.

Over time, the space between our thoughts expands from a millisecond to a second, to longer. We don't need to *try* to do it. If we practice the cycle during our meditation rather than following each thought that comes, it will happen without us forcing at all.

If we keep practicing, then someday, maybe, we can stay in the gap as long as our dogs.

I opened another eye and gazed at Maui. She looked like she was in total peace.

I sighed. Her peacefulness reminded me of the ultimate reason I meditate.

BLISS

Bliss isn't an effervescent happiness that gives us the ability to levitate or walk on water.

Bliss is a by-product of the cycle; it is the sum of the time we spend in the gap.

Most dogs have bliss — lots of it.

Maui stretched on my lap and rolled onto her back. She gazed up at me in that satisfied, uncomplicated way that dogs do when they are at one with the world. Her look said that she was thrilled to have me as pack leader and happy to keep going along with the experience of sharing her life with me.

I rubbed her stomach, smiling at her with a little bliss of my own.

Bliss is the deep satisfaction we feel when endorphins are abundant. The more time we spend in the gap, the more our body signals our brain to stop production of stress hormones, and to secrete calming hormones like endorphins and serotonin.

Admittedly, some meditation days are more bliss-filled than others, and so we can't count on a steady compounding of bliss each day we progress in our meditation.

Meditation is like jogging. A person rarely gets that runner's high their first time out — though it is possible. But, just as the more often we jog the more we are likely to experience that runner's high, the more we meditate, the more likely we are to experience bliss.

Maui yawned and stretched again. I stretched, too. She licked my face.

"Okay, girl, thanks for indulging me," I said.

She seemed to smile, as if happy to have shared the experience.

I bet that your dog will be happy to share it, too. All it takes to find out is to give it a try.

Just the Bones

Bone by Bone

- **Decide to Do It:** Set your intention.

- **Set the Stage:** Find a place to sit, put on music, etc.

- **Get Your Dog:** Bring your dog to the place you have chosen to meditate.

- **Return to Intention:** Reaffirm your intention to meditate

- **Synch:** Synchronize your breath with your dog's.

- **The Cycle:** Observe that you are having a thought, let it go, and return to synch.

By following these steps you'll spend some time in the gap, which is the space between thoughts. The more time you spend in the gap, the more you will experience bliss —just like your dog.

"If there are no dogs in heaven, then when I die I want to go where they went."

~ Unknown

CHAPTER 5

When Your Dog Won't Meditate with You

It happens.

It even happens to Maui and me.

Dogs are individuals; they have moods.

One of Maui's recurrent mood changes involves her favorite game—fetch. She goads me into throwing the ball, and for a while all is well. But now and then, about the ninth throw, she stares at me blankly, like my throwing the ball is the most inane thing she's seen, and she walks away leaving me to fetch.

Maui likes meditation even more than she likes to play fetch, but she still sometimes gets fidgety, or decides that meditation is not what she wants to do.

The first thing to remember is that meditation should not be a battle of wills. But neither should we let our dogs' proclivities run the show.

Let's go back to our meditation room for a moment and replay one of the times that Maui decided she didn't want to meditate.

I was sitting in my chair and Maui was sitting on my lap. All was well at first, and then she turned restless. She tried to stand—which she does only when she is going to jump off my lap.

I moved both my hands to her low back and gently held her backside down. She wiggled a bit then settled back into her hound-lounge.

If your dog is large or is lying nearby rather than on your lap, the idea is the same. When he tries to get up, gently press his haunches back down.

The first time we try to hold our dogs down during meditation can feel weird—it certainly did for me. But dogs are anxious to please us. More often than not, they will do what we want them to do—as long as they know what we are asking.

Gently pushing a dog's haunches back to the ground signals to the dog that we want him to keep lying down. If we do this consistently, our dogs will eventually learn to stay put during meditation.

Be patient. New skills take time. Harry Houdini taught his Terrier, Bobby, to escape ropes and handcuffs. But I bet Bobby didn't catch on during the first try.

Even when dogs like meditation, they may, at times, choose not to participate.

This time Maui was determined. She squirmed again under my hands, twisted free, and then leapt from my lap.

I kept my eyes shut and returned my focus to my breath.

It does us no good to fret or get angry if our dogs wiggle away. Speculating on why the dog left can plunge us into the cycle and interfere with our meditation.

Whatever the reason the dog left, if we stay calm and focused, the pooch will usually return.

"First my ball rolled under the sofa, then my water dish was too warm, then the squeaker broke on my squeaky rubber pork chop. I've had a horrible day and I'm completely stressed out!!!"

Our dogs *want* to be near us. The physical closeness of meditation is reminiscent of dogs lounging with their pack.

I heard Maui's tags jingle as she walked a few feet away and plopped on the floor. I continued breathing deeply, not wondering why she got up, or worrying if she would return. I knew she would.

There have been times when I was done with my meditation before Maui returned, and that's okay. We want to habituate our dogs to the joy of meditation, not make it a chore.

As we and our dogs experience more time in synch and synergy, our pooches are less likely to separate from us during meditation.

After a few minutes, I heard Maui's tags rattle again and she jumped back onto my lap, laid down, and fell right into her hound-lounge.

I rubbed behind her ear to let her know that I was glad she was back and that we could finish our meditation together.

If we are persistent and consistent with the signals we give our dogs, they should come to welcome meditation time.

Are there some dogs who simply can't meditate?

Personally, I don't think so. Meditation is a natural state for dogs. I have never worked with a dog who was ultimately unwilling to meditate. But some dogs, particularly dogs who have been abandoned or abused, or are unusually aggressive or hyper, have something standing between them and their true inner dog.

The process of helping these dogs find their inner dog requires what I call active compassion, known in human circles as tough love. In the appendix at the back of the book is a section on active compassion. There is also an article about active compassion on the website: www.DogMeditation.com.

If a dog doesn't take to meditation, don't give up. It's often the dogs who resist meditation that need it the most.

Just the Bones

When Your Dog Won't Meditate with You

- Gently hold your dog's haunches down when he tries to get up.

- If your dog does leave meditation, stay relaxed and meditate on your own. Your dog will likely return.

- When your dog returns, give a gentle acknowledgement that you are glad that he is back.

- If your dog doesn't return, try again next time. Sometimes it takes a dog a while to catch on, and sometimes dogs are not in the mood to meditate.

- Remember, meditation should be a joy for a dog, not a chore.

"*Dogs need to sniff the ground. It's how they keep abreast of current events. The ground is a kind of giant dog newspaper, containing all kinds of late-breaking dog news items, if they are especially urgent, they are often continued on the next lawn.*"

~ Dave Barry, Humorist & Writer

CHAPTER 6

Walking Meditation

When we meditate with our dogs, we bond with them as well as reap the benefits of meditation for ourselves. But walking meditation is true multitasking: we bond with our dogs, meditate, *plus* get some exercise.

The key to walking meditation is to embrace the present moment—the sights, sounds, and smells that we usually screen out.

Maui tottered into the living room, where I was munching pretzels and sneaking in an afternoon movie.

"Hi, Maui," I said. I wiped off my pretzel hand and gave her a pat on the head, but kept my eyes on the TV screen.

Maui danced a circle in the middle of the floor, tags jingling into the movie's dialogue.

I looked at her. "What?"

She stopped a moment, gazed up at me, her eyes intent. Then she went back to dancing her circle, adding a whimper every few seconds.

"You have to go *now*?"

She yelped and ran to the door.

I turned off the tv, then followed her to the door and let her out into the front yard.

Maui wandered the yard, sniffing here and there—and here again—as if the exact geocentric location she chose could stave off the melting of the polar ice caps. Finally, she christened the grass and sprinkled the corner brick that bordered the shrubbery bed. She ran up the steps to the house, but stopped at the far side of the porch. I stood aside so that she could come in. She barked and ran back down the steps.

I sighed. "Come on, Maui, I'm in the middle of something. We'll walk later."

But she was already at the end of the drive-way, sniffing out the route.

Oh well, I could use the exercise. I grabbed a couple of plastic bags and her leash, which I shook so she could see it. She came running.

"All right, Maui. You win," I said as I clipped the leash onto her collar. "We'll take a *short* walk."

Maui strained against the leash as I walked down the steps, and then she charged from yard to yard.

When Maui first came to live with me, I was a little self-conscious each time we went for a walk. Don't think that I haven't had my share of grief being a six-foot tall guy with an itty-bitty dog.

Truth is, I had a girlfriend once who had a Maltese, and I fell in love—with the breed. The girlfriend and I didn't work out. But when things ended and it came time for me to get a dog, I went out and got the feistiest, most lionhearted Maltese that I could find. Maui may be small, but she believes that she's the King Kong of dogs.

Like I said though, in the beginning, walking with a tiny, four-legged fluff ball got me a lot of puzzled looks.

The nice thing about turning an ordinary walk into a walking meditation is that the looks don't matter. I don't even see them anymore because I'm meditating.

As Maui pulled on, I took a few deep breaths and began my meditation. First, I focused on the feel of my breath as it entered and exited my lungs.

In some ways, walking meditation seems the antithesis of seated meditation—we are moving, our eyes are open, we stay alert to our surroundings, and we explore our senses one by one.

But much of the process is the same. We choose a focal point—in this example, we'll focus on sensation rather than synch. When we find our minds wandering, we'll refocus on the chosen sense.

I like to start with the feel of my breath because when I'm outdoors and exerting myself, breath feels so much different than it does when I meditate indoors.

The first thing I noticed on this walk was that the air was rain damp, as if a drizzle sat just past the horizon. I pulled the wet air into my lungs and savored its freshness.

Maui tugged against the leash as she pressed ahead. Maui's walking meditation focused predominately on the sense of smell, and she seemed to have caught the scent of Hypre, the cat belonging to my neighbor, who was such a prized feline that his name was painted on the mailbox. Hypre sat atop the mailbox, his tail whisking back and forth toward the ground in a lazy tease of my tiny, though dauntless, dog.

Maui ran for the mailbox, barking up a storm. Hypre sat so unperturbed that I wondered if he was meditating.

I pulled Maui away from what I knew from experience would be a frustrated thwarting of Maui's intention.

"Come on, girl," I said as I tugged her away.

Grand Avenue: © United Feature Syndicate, Inc.

"It's just not going to happen, there are just some things that you have to accept."

Maui glared at Hypre and gave the cat a few more ear-piercing barks.

I finally got her back on track with our walk. Walking meditation isn't always smooth. The trick is that when a distraction is over, we move right back into meditation.

I refocused on my breath as Maui and I continued along the sidewalk. I had to quicken my pace to keep up with her and soon felt a shift in my breath. It became faster and more shallow as our walk turned more aerobic.

I almost tripped over Maui as she halted in front of Mrs. Turner and her immaculate garden.

Uh oh. Mrs. Turner's rosebushes were a favorite place for Maui to make a deposit—especially when Mrs. Turner was in her yard. Maui loved an audience.

I tugged at the leash to veer Maui away from the yard—and save Mrs. Turner a sensory experience that I was sure she would rather not have.

Maui looked up at me, her eyes cross at my foiling her plan.

"Sorry Maui," I whispered. "Not today."

I smiled as I pulled Maui along and exchanged pleasantries with Mrs. Turner. Once we were a few houses away, Maui went back to her sniffing, while I decided to shift my focus from breathing to touch.

I started with my feet and the way they felt in my shoes as they rolled from heel to toe. I noticed, too, the way the cracks in the cement felt different beneath my feet than the sidewalk's flat surface.

As I moved my awareness up my body, I noticed that my knees absorbed the shock of each step more so than did my hips. My arms prickled against a light breeze. I felt the sun heat my face much more than it did my scalp, which was protected by hair.

Maui barked, snapping me out of my meditation. It wasn't a fierce bark, though. It was a friendly one.

I looked around, and saw a Schnauzer leading an older woman in the direction of the dog park.

Maui seemed to be saying a cordial, "I'll see you there."

"This was supposed to be a *short* walk, Maui," I said.

But she dashed on as if she hadn't heard, and I followed, enjoying both the meditation and the walk.

I decided to shift my focus to smell, so that I could move past it to something else *before* we got to the dog park. Concentrating on that particular sense, in that particular place, could result in sensory overload.

I glanced at Maui to see if I could learn anything about the sensory experience of smell. She was obviously good at it, running as she did from smell to smell like a detective following a fast-paced series of leads.

She was most interested in ground smells. In particular, the scents in places strategically important to dogs—fire hydrants, tree trunks, leafy plants that straddled the space between driveways and lawns.

She was rapt in the scents, I could tell. But I supposed that even if I could smell what she smelled, I wouldn't find them nearly as pleasing as she did.

I turned my attention to the first scent caught by my human nose—the sweet smell of Mr. Inue's freshly cut grass.

The scent reminded me of summers playing in the park as a child, and of my weekend chores as a teenager. I saw myself—

"We are having a thought," the observer noted.

Oops. I smiled as I let the thought go, and returned my attention to smell— plumeria blossoms that evoked an image of a vast tropical garden, the faint whiff of garbage from a overflowing can across the street.

Hmmm. Time to change senses. Sight, that's a good one.

It's worth mentioning here that walking meditation is as unique as seated meditation. For me, concentrating on the breath and the senses works best, but you might find another focal point that works better for you.

I focused on sight as Maui and I pressed on.

After noticing each crack in the sidewalk as we passed, and admiring the way the sidewalk wove so perfectly between the curving street and adjacent yards, I focused on sound. I identified at least three different pitches of bird chirping, heard the dull roar of traffic on the main road, and then eavesdropped for a short moment on a cell phone conversation of a woman pushing twins in a stroller.

I smiled and nodded as the trio passed, and pulled Maui gently away from the stroller as she tried to get a better whiff of the twins. It didn't take much to divert her attention from the stroller, though, as around the next corner was the dog park.

She yelped and strained against the leash as we approached. Once there, I let her loose so that she could assert her alpha personality on the large dogs, who often let her pretend that she's in charge.

She ran off barking and then muscled a resting Retriever into play.

I sat on a bench, relaxed, and let my full surroundings drift into sensory awareness.

The sunshine warmed my skin. The sound of frolicking dogs brought a smile to my face. In the peace of that moment, my mind became quiet.

Each moment passed into the next without great event—just me sitting alone on a bench at a dog park. But the sights and sounds of the dog park cascaded through me. I felt as if I were truly *there*, and yet, not there at all, almost as if I had become one with everything that surrounded me.

It was a moment of bliss in the midst of the mundane.

I smiled wider. This was why I meditated each day.

I thought for a moment about how much we missed out on when our minds focused on something other than the here and now.

Then I turned my attention to Maui and watched her romp with the other dogs.

She snatched a tennis ball away from a German Shepherd and started a game of chase. She coaxed a shy puppy into play by gently nipping at his tail. I cringed as she nudged the shoulder of a persnickety Bulldog so she could claim part of his shady place to sit.

Maui played so hard that when she came back, she had no energy to jump onto the bench next to me.

I reached down and lifted her up.

"Did you have a good time, girl?" I said

She answered by yawning, crawling onto my lap, lying down, and promptly closing her eyes. She fell asleep immediately.

"Yeah," I said. "So did I."

I had, and I was grateful again for a guru dog that knew just the right moment to coax me out for a walk.

I clipped her leash back on, which usually roused her enough for the walk home. But not this time.

She was exhausted.

Her present moment was one of rest, and she snuggled further into my lap.

She didn't flinch when I picked her up and cuddled her under my arm. She knew from past experience that I would carry her home.

Just the Bones

Walking Meditation

- In both walking and seated meditation, the object is to keep your attention on your chosen focal point and to return your mind to the focal point whenever you become distracted.

- Walking meditation is different than seated meditation in that your eyes are open, you're moving around, and the focal point may be different.

- Focal points during walking meditation include, but are not limited to, the breath and the five senses. Play around with a variety of focal points and see what works best for you.

Digging Deeper: Meditation for Pack Leaders

"Dogs are our link to paradise... to sit with a dog on a hillside on a glorious afternoon is to be back in Eden, where doing nothing was not boring — it was peace."

~ Milan Kundara, Author

CHAPTER 7

Treats for Pack Leaders

As promised in the first chapter, there are a lot of special meditation benefits for pack leaders. If you've begun meditating, then you might have experienced some of them. If you haven't yet tried meditation, then here's a preview of what you can look forward to.

The benefits of meditation for pack leaders tend to be progressive—from the concrete to the more ephemeral.

Maui yawned as she lay next to my leg. I sat on the floor with my laptop on the coffee table, typing a business letter. Next to Maui was a plastic newspaper that she liked to chase—when the bliss-disc or an ordinary ball wouldn't do. She'd brought it to me hoping for a game, but I had to finish my letter. So she acquiesced this time and stretched out for a hound-lounge, demonstrating the first benefit that pack leaders—and dogs—get from meditation.

RELAXATION

When we meditate, we quiet our minds, breathe slowly, and let go of the thoughts that race through our heads.

The most immediate effect of this process is relaxation. Our heart rates decrease, our blood pressures drop, our anxieties ease. All this can happen after just a few minutes of meditation.

Maui's ears twitched as if punctuating the previous point.

I smiled. Even in hound-lounge, she brought me joy. Just being around her gave me a sense of peace.

But that should come as no surprise. Studies have shown what dog lovers have known for years—that sharing our lives with dogs has a calming effect on our psyches. It improves our health and makes life more enjoyable.

In fact, many of the benefits of having a dog are similar to the benefits of meditation.

Paw in paw with the effect of mental relaxation is the physical benefit of:

STRESS RELIEF

Of course, Maui has her share of "accidents" on the carpet, of midnight wake-up barks at the shadows of trees, and there is the occasional aerobic challenge of corralling Maui into one of those pet travel carriers.

But for me, life with Maui more than compensates for these minor stresses. There's nothing that quite matches the feeling when I come home and she is there to greet me.

Both meditation and living with a dog improve a pack leader's health. Studies have shown that meditation can lower blood pressure and heart rate, decrease stress hormones, increase endorphins, and relieve pain.

Other things that I've noticed in both Maui and myself are more agreeable dispositions, an increased sense of security, freer self-expression, and increased playfulness.

Maui sat up, suddenly perky after her hound-lounge. She stood, jumped on my lap, and stared at the flowing prose on the screen. Then she yelped excitedly as her front paws sprang onto the keyboard.

cmmcdknckcmdkxmklmkddkmxkmkdkxlk —

"Maui!" I lifted her off of the keyboard. "What are you doing?"

I was about to put her outside — where she could do no more harm — when I caught myself.

I took a deep breath, then another.

Then I mumbled, mantra-like, "Objectivity. Objectivity. Objectivity."

OBJECTIVITY

Objectivity is the practice of stepping out of the immediacy of a situation or emotion and looking at it, well, objectively.

I glanced at Maui, and then at her crazy word at the end of my business letter. I laughed.

After all, what would it take to reverse what she had done? A single click of the undo function? Or maybe a quick highlight and delete?

I hugged Maui to me.

She gave a congenial *arf*.

Objectivity doesn't come quite as quickly as relaxation or stress relief, but it is something we cultivate during meditation that will eventually carry over into other areas of our lives.

Objectivity is a great benefit in itself, but there's a bonus that comes as a result of objectivity.

COMPASSION

I scratched behind Maui's ears. She looked at me a little suspiciously, this loving scratch on the heels of my little outburst.

"Objectivity inspires compassion, Maui," I said.

She gazed up at me as if this was old news to her.

Dogs embody compassion.

A friend once told me about a half-wild dog he adopted while in the Peace Corps. One day my friend had an accident that nearly ripped off his big toenail. It was bleeding badly and he had no way to stop it right that moment. The dog was with him, and without hesitation the dog began to lick the wound the way my friend had seen the dog do to injured dogs. Yes, it might have been instinct, but the dog had been around other familiar people when they were injured, and he had not reacted the same way. So my friend was convinced that the dog was showing compassion for him the same way he showed it for the canine members of his pack.

For humans, compassion is the art of being gentle and loving, of embracing objectivity, invoking patience, and exercising forgiveness. We pack leaders usually get to practice a lot of compassion by living with dogs.

Maui stared up at me, then looked toward the floor at the plastic newspaper that lay, still un-played-with, next to her.

I chuckled. I imagined that Maui exercised a lot of patience and forgiveness living with me, too.

"Okay, Maui," I said. I grabbed the newspaper chew-toy and tossed it.

Maui dashed from under the table, snatched the toy from its landing place, then dropped it next to my hand, yapping excitedly to spur me into throwing the newspaper once more.

I threw it again, telling myself that the business letter could wait — I was living in the moment.

LIVING IN THE MOMENT

Dogs live in the present moment.

When Maui has a liver treat, she is a hundred percent focused on it. When I pet her, she laps up the love. Whatever the present moment holds for her, she is in it.

I, on the other hand, am in the present moment in body, but my mind is often occupied with things like re-scripting a previous conversation — to my advantage of course, or wondering

"And only you can hear this whistle?"

what to have for dinner, or whether the weekend would be a good one to learn how to windsurf, or debating whether windsurfing was really a wise idea, or…well, you get the picture.

Keeping the mind centered on the present moment is difficult. Meditation helps us practice staying in the present, which, if we think about it, is the only moment we have.

Maui ran back with the plastic newspaper. I picked it up, tossed it again. She chased it and brought it back. This game, I knew, could go on for hours.

Most dogs chase things that move. It's their instinctive response.

Humans have instinct, too, but we call it:

INTUITION

Intuition is a powerful benefit of meditation.

Maui brought the toy back, dropped it, and yelped in the direction of the computer, which was occupying my throwing hand.

I reached down and tossed the newspaper.

Maui scurried after it.

Dogs rely on and hone their instinct throughout their lives—they know when earthquakes will strike, or when their pack leaders are soon to return to the pack. Stories abound about dogs left a thousand miles from home who have found their way back without a map or GPS.

Like dog instinct, human intuition is naturally present in everyone. We often call intuition that "little voice."

When our minds are cluttered the "little voice" is hard to hear. Or, if we hear it, we do not pay attention.

The "little voice" that suggests that we might be better off driving home the scenic way often gets overruled by the voice of the rational mind that says we should drive home directly so as not to lose time. Self-doubt squelches the "little voice" when it announces that we are silly to believe every errant thought that springs to mind. It can also be drowned out by the noise that invades our lives—the cell phone, radio and TV, the list goes on.

The inner stillness we cultivate in meditation helps us reach beneath these distractions so that we can better hear and trust our intuitive voice.

Maui returned once more with her newspaper, and dropped it, wagging her tail.

"Okay, girl," I said. "But this is the last time for now."

I threw. She chased and brought it back. I took it from her and tapped it a few times on the ground—my signal to her that our playtime was done.

She pouted for a moment, then plopped to the ground, yawned and settled herself down for a nap.

CONTENTMENT

As long as Maui is fed, has a place to sleep, a certain amount of attention, and some grass on which to relieve herself, she is content.

That's not to say that she doesn't have desires. In fact, she has a lot of them.

"Steak," I said softly.

Maui's head popped up, she sniffed the air, and then looked at me quizzically.

"Maybe we'll have steak for dinner," I said.

Maui wagged her tail. She loves steak. She drools from the moment the package makes an appearance on the counter, but she doesn't need steak to make her happy. She has an inner state of contentment.

We develop this same sort of state through meditation.

Contentment is not complacency. We all have goals—the perfect job, a better house, a stronger body. But there is a difference between needing these things in order to be content, and maintaining a state of contentment while in pursuit of our dreams.

With no steak materializing, Maui jumped up and attacked her plastic newspaper. She chewed it with such gusto that I thought by sheer persistence she might be able to tear it to shreds.

I waved my hand over her head, then in front of her eyes, but she wasn't giving in to distraction. She was concentrating, zoned in on a single purpose.

FOCUS

If your dog is anything like Maui, then when she is chewing a toy, she's lost in the chewing; when the doorbell rings, the most important thing in her world is to bark at the person on the other side of the door; and when it's meal time, the house could collapse around her but it won't chase her from her food.

We may shake our heads at this single-mindedness, but it is a gift, as well as an eventual benefit of meditation.

We all have some ability to focus. Without any, we would be unable to live orderly lives. But how many of us keep our total concentration on the road when driving a familiar route, or when carrying on an extended conversation with a four year-old?

We split our focus because these situations don't require our full attention. That doesn't mean we shouldn't give it—accidents happen most often to distracted drivers, and the discourse of young children can contain surprising nuggets of wisdom.

In meditation, we practice re-focusing the mind when our thoughts drift. This helps us think more clearly, eliminate cluttering thoughts, and stay engaged in the moment—whether that moment is in meditation, in work, or roaring in laughter.

I reached down and tickled Maui under her chin. She looked up, then abandoned the newspaper, and jumped onto my lap. Her big brown eyes beamed from under a curl of hair that looked like exaggerated false-eyelashes.

She licked at my jaw—a request for a snack.

But instead of running to the kitchen, Maui gazed at me a moment, then circled around in my lap, lay down and eased into her hound-lounge, as if certain that if she stayed peaceful and patient, food would come.

This was not one of Maui's ploys for food — I knew them all. This was what I thought of as Maui's true state of being.

ENLIGHTENMENT

Enlightenment is the most ephemeral of the benefits that we talk about here.

The exact meaning of enlightenment is debated by those hoping to achieve it, and spoken about metaphorically by those who have.

Enlightenment doesn't mean that we don't get angry, or that when we step on a tack it doesn't hurt.

Enlightenment does not disengage us from the world. In fact, just the opposite is true.

Enlightened beings are engaged with the world because they live in the present moment. They do not worry about the future or fret about the past.

There is no magic mantra that leads to enlightenment; it can't be conferred from one person to another.

It's elusive, though we get glimpses of it as we meditate—and when we practice the life we learn from our dogs.

Just the Bones

Treats for Pack Leaders

Some of the benefits of meditation for humans are:

- Relaxation
- Stress Relief
- Objectivity
- Compassion
- Living in the Moment
- Intuition
- Contentment
- Focus
- Enlightenment

"I think we are drawn to dogs because they are the uninhibited creatures we might be if we weren't certain we knew better."

~ George Evans, Author, "Troubles With Bird Dogs"

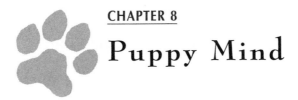

CHAPTER 8

Puppy Mind

Daily meditation can transform our lives.

When we consistently practice the cycle, which we discussed in the third chapter, Bone By Bone, we cultivate awareness. Once we become more aware of our thoughts, we can alter negative or destructive thoughts more easily.

Maui ran into the dining room and then in three circles around my chair. I reached out my leg to see if I could slow her down, but she just jumped over my foot and kept running—twice more around the chair then back out the door.

Hmmm. Had I fed her anything different this morning? Not that I could remember.

I shrugged and turned back to my newspaper.

Maui charged back into the room, trailing a long banner of toilet paper.

"Maui, what are you doing?"

She yelped and ran a figure eight on the dining room floor. She dropped the toilet paper from her mouth, ran out, and scampered back in with a piece of toilet paper so long that it rounded the corner into the hallway…did she have it strung all the way from the bathroom?

I opened my mouth to reprimand her, but I cracked up laughing instead. She was just too comical to scold.

I took a piece of scratch paper, wadded it into a ball, and threw it over her head—scratch paper balls usually kept her occupied for a good ten minutes.

Maui abandoned the toilet paper and pounced on the ball. She had it shredded in under a minute, then looked up, as if searching out something else to destroy.

I wadded another scratch paper ball—which lasted her maybe a minute and a half.

She spit out the last slobbery bits of paper, then looked around and spied my shoes.

"Oh no you don't," I said. I snatched her up in my hand as I walked toward the door.

"You know what your problem is, Maui?" I said. "You're trapped in puppy mind."

She looked up at me, her brown eyes squeezed in question.

"Your attention bounces from one thing to another like a hyperactive puppy," I said in explanation.

She gave me a doggy frown.

I sighed. Sometimes I forgot that in dog years, she was decades older than me.

"You don't have to be a puppy to have puppy mind, Maui," I said. "In fact, you don't even need to be a dog."

I carried her past the streamers of toilet paper and into the kitchen. In the drawer was a red plastic ball that she loved to chase so much that I hid it in the off time so as not to be trapped into never-ending games of fetch.

101

I took out the ball and rolled it across the floor. Maui went after it as if it were made of sirloin. She chased it until it was trapped between the cupboard and the floor.

She turned her head sideways and tried to pull it loose with her teeth, but it wouldn't budge. She stood back and glared at the ball.

Gruuuuufff!

"Chill out, Maui."

Maui looked up as I said her name, her gape expectant, as if willing something important to happen—snacks, a walk, a new toy. When nothing pertinent materialized, she turned her attention back to the ball.

Gruuuuufff!

"Take a deep breath, Maui," I said. "And relax."

She took another swipe or two at the ball, then must have caught sight of the toilet paper, because off she went in that direction.

I kicked the ball free as I called her name. She dashed back and grabbed the ball, and I resigned myself to a long game of fetch to settle her down.

I walked into the living room, sat on the floor, and leaned back against the couch.

Maui brought the ball to me, dropped it, and barked—her demand that I take up my role as pitcher in the game.

I threw the ball across the room. She brought it back. This went on for a while, and I began to curse puppy mind.

But was I any better?

I had enough awareness to admit that I wasn't.

In puppies and small children, puppy mind is cute. That never-ending shift of attention at every stimulus reminds us that when we are new to the world, everything is fresh and exciting.

As we get older, an easily distracted mind becomes a burden, especially when it asserts that we are "less than" or "not enough."

While puppy mind is irritating in us pack leaders, a constant stream of *negative* puppy mind is downright destructive.

© 2002 Kristine Neddersen from kyotedog.com

I threw the ball a few more times for Maui, thankful that *human* puppy mind doesn't require endless games of fetch to tame.

For humans, puppy mind is all in the head.

The first step in countering puppy mind is awareness: before we can change puppy mind, we need to be aware that we are in its grip.

Maui ran back for the umpteenth time and dropped the ball near my hand. She looked no more tired than when we started.

"Guess what, Maui," I said as I picked up the ball. "I'm going to make this a workout for me, too. A *mind* workout."

Maui seemed uninterested in what I was saying—she had her gaze firmly fixed on the ball.

I tossed. She chased.

To counter human puppy mind, we utilize the same cycle that we use during meditation, but with two key differences.

The first difference is focal point.

In meditation, we focus on synch.

During our non-meditation time, the focal point is whatever we have our attention on—in my case, on the red ball and the game with Maui.

I paid attention to the game as best as I could, and tossed the ball when she brought it back. For a few minutes, both of us were engrossed in the fate of the little red ball.

Then it happened.

I remember reading somewhere that dogs are bred to remain playful throughout their lives. It's a good thing, too. Could you imagine a stodgy old wolfhound with a proverbial pipe and smoking jacket, wiling away the time playing chess for liver snacks with the aging poodle next door...?

"We are having a thought," the observer said.

Puppy mind had bounded in.

If we were in meditation, we would gently let go of the thought. But outside of meditation, the observer can get a little more loquacious—actually examining the thought and its relevance to the situation.

This expanded role of the observer is the second key difference between how we use the cycle during meditation and how we use it when countering puppy mind.

"Funny," the observer continued, "How our minds tend to think *about* what we are doing rather than focusing *on* what we are doing."

True statement, I acknowledged, and a nugget of wisdom besides.

I let go of the thought and turned my attention to Maui. I tried to focus on our game—the feel of the ball in my hand, the deft techniques I had developed of throwing it, the way it bounced off an empty coffee cup that I had left on a coaster on the floor...

Hmmm, what's that empty coffee cup doing there? And what's in it? Had it been there so long that it was coated with the moldy remains of cream and half-dissolved sugar? No, it would have dried and cracked by now, it's been at least a week. A week? Uh oh, am I a slob...?

"Oddly enough I'm indifferent about
the UPS guy."

"We are having a thought," the observer observed. "A *negative* thought."

Yikes, I was. I sighed. Negative puppy mind is a hard habit to break. But becoming aware of negative puppy mind is the first step.

When we are aware we're having a negative thought, we can examine it, challenge it, then alter it.

Altering a thought helps us transform a negative thought into a supportive, non-judgmental truth.

"Yes, I had left out a coffee cup, but it's not my usual habit," I restated. "Forgetting to pick up a coffee cup does not make me a slob. After all, I left it on a coaster."

I felt better already.

I brought my attention back to the ball, and tossed it down the hall, trying to focus on the sound of Maui as she bounded after it—the tinkling tags, her excited yelps, her happy puppy-like pants as she chased...

Observing the mind is a fun, fairly simple, activity—like watching a puppy play. Observation breeds awareness, and once we are aware, it is only a matter of altering our thoughts to change our thinking patterns...

"We are having a thought," the observer observed. "A pontificating thought."

"Quiet," I said, trying to ignore the observer.

Sometimes I enjoy pontificating.

"We are still having the thought," the observer said.

"Right," I said half-heartedly, still caught up in puppy mind.

Hey, aren't you listening? Here you are pontificating about the insidiousness of puppy mind and yet you're letting your inner puppy run the show.

"Ahem," the observer said. "We are still—"

"Yes, I know," I said.

"Just checking," the observer said.

Fair enough.

Then I did what I knew I should do—I let go of the thought.

It's hard to resist the temptation to follow interesting thoughts. But when we refocus the mind rather than letting puppy mind frolic, we maximize the benefits of meditation for pack leaders.

How?

Well, the more we invoke—and listen to—the observer the more we cultivate objectivity, and, ultimately, compassion.

Using the observer to become aware of our thoughts and examine them helps us distinguish the voice of intuition from random thoughts that pop into our heads. Once we identify the intuitive voice, and learn to act on its suggestions, we will see our intuitive abilities flourish.

Gently pulling our minds away from distractions helps develop focus. The ability to focus keeps us living in the moment, and can help us alter the assertions of negative puppy mind.

A quieter, more focused mind fosters contentment, as it is less apt to be carried away by puppy mind, judgmental thoughts, and overreaction.

If we refocus our minds each time they stray, then staying focused eventually becomes a natural state, and we are immediately aware when our attention wanders.

Speaking of focus, I glanced down at my hand—and the ball that was still in it. I'd stopped throwing when my mind began to wander.

Generally, Maui had little patience for my wandering mind in the midst of a game. Usually, if the observer didn't catch me first, Maui brought my attention right back.

I looked around for Maui.

She was curled up under the table, her puppy mind was finally tuckered out.

Just the Bones

Puppy Mind

- The tendency of the human mind to jump from one random thought to another is similar to a puppy in play, and can be trained.

- You can counter puppy mind by using the cycle when you find your mind wandering—become aware that you are distracted, let go of the distracting thought, and return your focus to the task at hand.

- The process of using the cycle to counter puppy mind in daily life—rather than just during meditation—further improves objectivity, compassion, intuition, contentment, focus, and the ability to live in the moment.

"Folks will know how large your soul is by the way you treat a dog."

~ Charles F. Doran, Author

CHAPTER 9

Learning to Sit on Command

If you've spent time training your dog, then you know the importance of associating the command you give with the action you are trying to get your dog to do.

That *aha* moment when a dog finally puts the command and the action together lights up his face, and you know he can then perform the command anytime you ask—unless your dog is like Maui.

Maui is smart, don't get me wrong. But there are times when she is a little too smart. Like when I taught her to roll over. She took to it quickly, but when I wanted to show it off to a friend, Maui just gazed up at me like I had lost my mind. It wasn't until I gave up (with my friend in stitches) that she rolled over and then walked away, laughing to her doggy self, I'm sure.

The process of association that we use when training a dog can work for us, too.

Maui romped into the room, then, seeing that I was working, she stretched in a yogic upward dog and downward dog, then turned around several times in a circle and sat down.

I smiled. I'd seen her do this before — it's her regular prelude to a nap.

Next, I knew, she would yawn, which would be followed by a faintly moaning yowl, then she'd flop to her side, turn onto her back and wiggle twice as if tending to an itch, then finally adopt her original lying down position and drift into her hound-lounge, and from there into sleep.

This is Maui's regular — and highly personal — ritual. She does this so consistently that I believe it's the way she signals her body that it's time to sleep.

Ritual is the process of using external gestures or symbols to induce an internal state.

Ritual is also a strategy we can use to signal our bodies and minds that it's time to meditate.

There is no real mystique about ritual. In fact, we already use ritual to effect internal states in various areas of our lives.

Here's one of mine:

I shower first thing in the morning most days. On the days I work or have some sort of professional or public endeavor, I end my shower with a long blast of cold water. The cold chases out any remnants of sleep, and the process alerts my body and mind that a day of work has begun. On the days I take long, steamy showers, my body and mind automatically shift into weekend mode.

This ritual may not apply to everyone, but we should all be able to think of something that sets the mood for the activity to come: the way we stare—wary or excited or with ambivalence—at our running shoes before lacing them up for a run; the act of putting on a favorite outfit as we get ready to go out on a Saturday night; the satisfaction of sliding back into bed with a steaming mug of fresh coffee and the Sunday paper.

Rituals are personal, and meditation is more personal still. It makes sense that the meditation rituals we adopt be meaningful to us—even if they aren't to anyone else.

The rituals we develop for ourselves will also help cue our dogs that it is time to meditate.

I have my favorite bathrobe, special music, and a particular chair that are part of Maui's and my meditation ritual. But play around to see what works best for you.

Some things to think about include:

SPACE

While we can meditate anywhere—watching a sunset on a beach, under a tree in a park, even in a train station—finding a peaceful space is key to setting the stage for a relaxing meditation. Ideally, we should find a place we can devote exclusively to meditation, whether it's a spare bedroom or a quiet corner of the living room.

One of Maui's favorite places to hound-lounge is curled up atop the fluffiest pillow on my bed. Wherever we choose, we want to designate it in our minds as a special place, so that when we go there, our bodies and minds are alerted that it's time to meditate.

TIME

Most meditation traditions stress the benefit of meditating first thing in the morning. It's the time when our minds and the world around us are most quiet, and our body is not yet keyed up for the action of the day. But meditation needs to fit into our schedules or we won't do it. More important than the actual time is that we try to meditate at the same time each day, whether it is mid-morning after the kids have gone to school, or in the late afternoon after work before we settle into our nightly activities. We want to choose a time that will work consistently for us. This repetition helps accustom our bodies and minds to meditate at a particular time. This habituation strengthens the power of our meditation ritual.

CLOTHING

I have my bathrobe, and some people have a favorite shirt or shawl. There isn't a strong tradition of using special clothing as part of meditation, but I've found that it helps me. Loose fitting, non-binding garments are more comfortable and make breathing easier.

Clothing has a powerful effect on mood. If in doubt, try going to work in a neon orange leisure suit and mismatched shoes. Special clothing can have an effect on our mindsets as we enter meditation. But like everything here, it is merely a suggestion—kibble for thought.

MUSIC

Music helps me focus, but for some people, it's a distraction. The kind of music we listen to during meditation is highly personal, too. Most meditation music is subdued, and might be filled with sounds from nature or distant bells. For some, this music works great. Others might like something more rhythmic, with instrumentals or even chanting.

Guided meditation, in which a narrator helps us focus on particular states or feelings, can also be helpful, especially for a new or highly distracted meditator.

To help beginning meditators, I'm offering a free CD with both my favorite meditation music and guided meditation. Details are in the appendix at the back of the book, as well as at www.DogMeditation.com.

SPECIAL PROPS

Many people like to meditate with their eyes closed, but those who don't might find it helpful to have a meaningful focal object to gaze at.

My favorite focal object is Maui—or more specifically, her ear or paw, or tail, whatever is most easily visible going into our meditation. More traditional props include: a burning candle, an item with religious significance such as a cross, a statue, or a picture of a beloved spiritual teacher. Be imaginative. The only criteria for special props are that they are significant to you.

Cartoon copyrighted by Mark Parisi, printed with permission.

SITTING ARRANGEMENTS

Whether we sit in a special chair or on the floor, we want to choose a sitting arrangement that is comfortable for both our dogs and us. Ideally, the spine should stay straight but not rigid, and we want to choose a position in which our legs and feet will not fall asleep or become cramped.

If we use a chair, it should be straight-backed enough that we are not inclined to slouch. If we are on the floor, a firm cushion can help make meditation more comfortable.

Dog cushions can easily double as meditation cushions, which is one more good reason to meditate in private—so that when we make ourselves comfy on our canines' cushion, the people around us won't think we've lost our minds.

I like to sit in the lotus position—cross-legged but with the feet on top of the thighs rather than underneath. Lotus position by nature allows us to sit with a straight spine for a long period of time—provided that lotus position is a comfortable position to hold. If it's not, try a regular cross-legged position, or sit on a chair with your feet flat on the floor. Lotus and other positions used in various meditation traditions are conventions rather than absolutes.

In fact, there are few rules, *per se*, about meditation.

The perfect meditation is whatever works best for you.

Just the Bones

Learning to Sit on Command

Ritual can help to signal you and your dog that it is time to meditate. Ritual is unique for each individual. Create rituals that are meaningful to you.

Some ideas include:

- Choose a consistent place to meditate.

- Meditate at the same time each day.

- Wear special, loose-fitting clothing.

- Play music.

- Use special prop—candles, pictures, religious objects, etc.

- Choose a comfortable place to sit, whether in a chair or on the floor.

"Humans have externalized their wisdom — stored it in museums, libraries, the expertise of the learned. Dog wisdom is inside the blood and bones."

~ Donald McCaig, Author

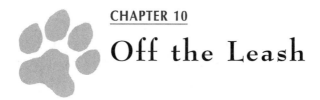

CHAPTER 10
Off the Leash

What if we love meditation so much that we want to bring it into other areas of our lives?

Or—what happens when we travel or are otherwise unable to share this special time with our dogs?

What do we do then?

Luckily, meditation has been a human practice for thousands of years and so there is a multitude of techniques.

Maui walked into the room, dragging a favorite blanket behind her. But instead of curling up at my feet like she usually does, she ambled to the dog blanket that I keep for her in a far corner of the room. She used her teeth and nose to move the blanket around just so, and then plopped down with a sigh.

"Hi, girl," I said.

She looked up at me. Her mouth opened a bit into a casual pant, but she didn't come over to greet me. Instead, she stayed on her blanket, and curled herself into a ball, which was her way of telling me that she wanted to be near, but that she wanted to do some hound-lounging on her own.

Fair enough. We all have our quirks — in life, and in meditation.

Since meditation is so personal, there are probably as many meditation techniques as there are meditators. I'll talk about five methods that can be adapted to suit individual tastes.

BREATH MEDITATION

Breath meditation is a lot like the meditation technique we used with our pooches.

It's synch, without the dog.

We sit quietly, close our eyes, and pay attention to the breath—the way it feels moving through the nose and lungs, the rise and fall of the chest and diaphragm, taking long, slow, deep inhales and relaxing further with each exhale.

When our attention wanders, we gently bring it back to our breath.

Simple, right?

The best part about it is that we can vary it to make it useful in numerous areas of our lives.

When we bring breath meditation off the meditation cushion, we use it the same way we did during walking meditation—remember?

We keep our eyes open and stay alert to our surroundings. We keep our attention on the breath and refocus on the breath when our mind wanders.

We can use breath meditation while folding clothes, washing dishes, standing in line at the supermarket, all sorts of activities.

Breath meditation has a profound calming effect on the body. Repeated slow, deep breathing signals the brain to reduce the secretion of stress hormones and to begin to secrete hormones like serotonin that help us relax.

This makes breath meditation a great thing to practice as we walk to a meeting that we know will be tense, or when stuck in traffic, or as we sit shivering in those paper gowns waiting for a doctor.

Try it for a few minutes and see how it works.

If you're like me, breath meditation is harder to stay focused on than the synch of Maui's breath and mine.

What do we do then?

In this case, we can adapt the breath meditation into:

BREATH COUNTING MEDITATION

There's no mystery behind breath counting meditation. It is exactly what it sounds like. In breath counting meditation, we keep our minds focused by counting the breaths as we exhale.

We can do a linear count—starting at one and going on from there. Or, if our minds are doggedly nomadic, we can make the counting a little more complex.

Another method is to count one to ten, then backward ten to one. Then count one to nine, then backward to one, and so on. When we reach one, we reverse the process: counting from one to two then back to one, then one to three then back to one, and so on back up to ten.

Ah, not a problem, you may be thinking. This breath counting meditation is a piece of cake.

Maybe, but the dog-hair-in-the-ointment of the practice is that, when our minds wander so far that we don't remember what number we are on, we don't get to guess, we have to start back at the beginning, with one.

SACRED WORD MEDITATION

Sacred word meditation is an adaptation of breath meditation—with a sacred twist. The nice thing is that the sacred part is individual.

We choose a word that is sacred to us. We can use the name of a religious figure like Jesus or Allah, a short phrase like Shalom, or the Hindu mantra *Om Namah Shivaya* (I surrender to God), or a more non-dogmatic words like love, or peace, or one.

When our minds wander, we gently let go of the intruding thought and then recite the word silently as we refocus on the breath.

Consider using the same sacred word each time. Over time, the sacred word itself helps us to relax as we come to associate it with the process of meditation and relaxation. This process of association works like the commands we use when training our dog.

Maui looked up and peered at me through the curl of hair above her eyes, as if remembering back to those days when we first explored the command "sit."

Maui likes commands — or rather, she likes words directed at her. She reacts as if in conversation, yapping back some quip to keep the banter going.

But "sit," which was the first command I tried to teach her, sparked confusion.

I think it was because the word was so short, unlike the chatty, "Good morning, Maui, what would you like for breakfast?" which always spurred a yap followed by a race to her food bowl.

"Sit" didn't prompt such an automatic response. It took three weeks of dog training to associate "sit" with the act of sitting.

The good news is that associating a sacred word with relaxation and deeper meditation should not be quite as arduous as Maui's learning to associate the word "sit" with the act of sitting. We choose the word, we know its meaning, and we know the intention.

The trick of associating a sacred word to meditation is that when we say the word, we do our best to refocus on the breath and the relaxation that deep breathing inspires.

SACRED VERSE MEDITATION

Sacred verse meditation is for those who don't want to limit themselves to a single sacred word.

Maui yawned and looked up at me, sleepy-eyed.

"Hmmm, Maui," I said. "If you had a sacred verse, what would it be?"

Maui tilted her head to one side, as if in thought.

"To err is human, to forgive, canine?" I said. "Or something equally profound from Snoopy or Marmaduke?"

Maui narrowed her gaze, as if frowning.

"Or are you more pragmatic?" I said. "Say, 'anytime is a good time for a nap?' or 'unlimited liver snacks for everyone?'"

Maui wagged her tail. I had found one that struck a chord.

Likewise, we can use whatever sacred verse appeals to us—long or short. It may be a favorite Psalm, or a passage from the Bhagavad Gita, the Gospels, or the Koran. We can choose a saying of a person we find wise — Archbishop Desmond Tutu, the Dalai Lama, even Oprah.

Or we can choose something we'd like to internalize, like the Golden Rule.

We can use the same sacred verse each time, or, unlike the sacred word, we can choose a new verse each time. Whatever we choose, we should have it memorized so that we don't have to break from meditation to look it up.

We should say the passage slowly, silently, focusing on each word, and pausing to allow quiet space between each word.

When we say our verse quickly — "Do-unto-others-as-you-would-have-them-do-unto-you-Do-unto-others-as-you-would-have-them-do-unto-you-Do-unto-others-as-you-would-have-them-do-unto-you..." we go on autopilot, which allows our minds to wander.

When we say each word slowly, it requires concentration. Honoring the space between words helps our minds to stay focused on the phrase rather than relying on rote memorization.

"Do unto others as you would have them do unto you," should take twenty or thirty seconds to say fully. When we spread out a phrase this short over that length of a time, it requires our full focus.

Oh, and when we stumble, we start again at the beginning.

CONSCIOUS ACTIVITY MEDITATION

Conscious activity meditation works best with simple or repetitive tasks like gardening, cooking, or even playing Solitaire, but it can be used with almost any activity.

I say "almost" because Maui very consciously chews out the footpads from my shoes when given the chance. Now, that may be a meditation to her, but I just can't bring myself to list it as such.

So one limit I like to put on this type of meditation is that the activity be useful or constructive.

Maui glanced around and spied the shoes I kicked off as I came in the door.

"Don't even think it, Maui," I said.

She looked away from the shoes and toward me, feigning guilelessness.

A few moments later, though, I saw Maui, inching her way across the carpet to my shoes.

"Maui," I said in a warning tone.

She stopped and then turned sheepish.

I sighed, wadded up a piece of scrap paper, and tossed it past her head. She hurtled after it, trapped it between her paws, and started tearing it to pieces.

I didn't like Maui chewing on my footpads, but, as far as conscious activity meditation was concerned, she had the perfect example—conscious eating.

In conscious eating meditation, we sit down to a meal—or to be fair, to a scratch paper ball or a tasty footpad—with the intention of focusing full attention on our food.

No TV, no newspaper by our plate, no dinnertime conversation. Just us and our food.

We focus for a moment on the food itself—
its color, the mix of ingredients, the nutrients
that will fuel our bodies.

We savor the aroma, sense our taste buds
readying, and feel the burst of saliva over our
tongues.

Then we focus on each action that goes into
eating—lifting the fork and knife, cutting our
food into pieces, scooping it up, and putting it
into our mouths.

We observe the taste and texture as we chew
our food, the feel of the food as we swallow, following the route from mouth to stomach.

We pause for a moment before focusing on
the next bite.

Whenever our minds wander, we gently
nudge them back to the experience of eating.

We can do this with a full meal, or with a
single raisin. If we do it with a raisin, I guaran-
tee that it will be the most flavor-filled raisin
that we ever eat.

Hmmm, I glanced at Maui, who was slowly shredding her paper ball and strewing pieces of it over the floor.

Does the act of staying focused make the scratch paper ball—or my footpads—taste extra good to her?

Probably, but only Maui knows.

Just the Bones

Off the Leash

It's easy to meditate without a dog, just use one of the following as a focal point rather than the synch of your breath and your dog's breath.

- 🦴 **Breath:** Focus on the feel of your breath entering and exiting your body.

- 🦴 **Breath Counting:** Focus on counting your breaths as you exhale.

- 🦴 **Sacred Word:** Use a sacred word to bring you back to focus when your mind wanders.

- 🦴 **Sacred Verse:** Say a special verse, such as a Psalm, slowly and silently using all of your focus.

- 🦴 **Conscious Activity:** Keep your focus on an easy activity like eating.

"With dogs, you don't need gurus. Dogs are forever in the moment. They are a tidal wave of feelings, and every feeling is a variant of love."

~ Cynthia Heimel, Columnist & Humorist

CHAPTER 11

Dog as Guru

Maui lay on her back on the floor. All four paws poked up in the air, and her teeth were bared in a contented grin.

Not exactly the stance we expect from a guru.

But she is. Your dog is, too.

Our dogs have amazing lessons to impart. These lessons are open to anyone who is willing to become a little less human and a little more dog.

Of course, each dog is different; each dog has his unique wisdom. But there are also some things that most dogs have in common.

Dogs can show us how to be better attuned to the rhythms of life: sleeping when we are tired, eating when we are hungry, playing when the opportunity arises or the mood strikes.

Most well-loved dogs are filled with trust and contentment. They know that they will be fed without needing to howl incessantly. They know that they will have a place to sleep, and are content whether they sleep on a hand-made, boutique dog cushion, or in a shady spot under a tree.

From dog nature, we learn to love what is around us. Dogs know innately that love creates energy, and to let go of fear and anger after a trauma passes.

Dogs flow with the present moment. From dogs we learn to take nothing personally, to hold no grudges. We learn to be quick to forgive and slow to growl.

Becoming more dog can give us a whole new leash on life.

If we watch our dogs, lessons abound. These are just a few of the things that Maui has taught me:

BARK AT FEAR

Maui is shorter and smaller than nearly everything around her. Yet, it's never seemed to occur to her that she is undersized. When she feels threatened, she never runs and hides. She barks, even snarls, in the face of her fear.

But she never barks any longer than she needs to. Once she is assured she is safe, she sniffs, wags her tail, and she makes friends with whatever frightened her. She lets fear go. She doesn't relive it by barking at the memory.

LIFE IS A BOWL OF LIVER SNACKS

Life is pleasure, but it's not about the pursuit of pleasure. It's about finding pleasure where we are. Dogs don't postpone happiness until they finagle one more treat, or until their human caretaker finds them a fancy sports car to ride around in.

Most dogs are happy where they are — and when circumstances improve, they will be happy there, too.

WHEN LIFE GIVES YOU DRY DOG FOOD, ADD WATER AND MAKE GRAVY

Life is quirky. Weird things happen, and some of them are downright unfair. Maui takes whatever happens in stride—even the occasional meal of dry dog food when I haven't had time to get to the store. She could growl, she could pout and hide under the bed, but she seems to know that good humor and an engaging wag of the tail go a lot further to buoying a situation.

When we take life too seriously, we rob ourselves of the inherent joy of present-moment living.

NEVER PASS UP A GOOD MEAL

When life offers Maui a feast, she eats, and so should we. Excessive calories and cholesterol warrant prudence in our daily habits, but when we become so obsessed that we can't let loose to take part in special occasions, we are clinging to the sort of rigidity that jeopardizes emotional and spiritual health.

WHEN SOMEONE COMES TO THE DOOR, WAG YOUR TAIL

Maui might bark and growl when a new person comes to the door, but as soon as that door opens, she wags her tail.

With her, visitors — even unexpected ones — bring joy to the day. She greets each visitor without reservation, even if they disturb her afternoon nap.

LOVE & LOOK OUT FOR YOUR PACK

My favorite place to watch Maui is in the dog park. She bonds immediately with most of the other dogs, and I can see in these fast-formed groups what canine pack life is like. They play together and bark with joy. They share the shade on hot days. On cold ones, they curl up together to keep each other warm. When one barks at something threatening, the others bark, too. They band together to keep each other and the pack safe and happy.

"*I actually know more commands than I respond to.*"

LICK THE ONES YOU LOVE

Maui never passes up a chance for a good snuggle. She jumps in my lap—or a visitor's lap—and makes herself at home. If there is no lap available, she brushes a leg or tries to wiggle her way under a hand for a pet. It's not a selfish pursuit, though. She always returns in kind with eager licking of her tongue. Yes, it can get messy, but it's the way she demonstrates love.

BE YOUR OWN DOG

Maui doesn't pretend to be anything other than a fluffy white Maltese with a good set of lungs. She might admire the long silky mane on the Afghan down the street, but she doesn't agonize in front of the mirror about her frizzy coat.

It's not, I believe, that she doesn't know any better. There are dozens of dogs she meets that are larger, louder, faster, or more showy. But Maui is fearless, and seems to know that it takes the most courage to be true to herself.

Maui opened her eyes, then rolled from her back onto her stomach and gazed up at me.

Then she sneezed.

"Are you trying to tell me something, Maui?" I said.

She looked at me a moment longer, then started nibbling the pads of her paw.

Maybe she was trying to teach me something, maybe she wasn't. She's not pedantic, so sometimes it's hard to tell. Her lessons are such a part of the way she lives, that I don't think she has to try at all.

She's a guru.

Just the Bones

Dog as Guru

Some lessons we learn from our dogs:

- Bark at fear.

- Life is a bowl of liver snacks.

- When life gives you dry dog food, add water and make gravy.

- Never pass up a good meal.

- When someone comes to the door, wag your tail.

- Love and look out for your pack.

- Lick the ones you love.

- Be your own dog.

"There is no psychiatrist in the world like a puppy licking your face."

~ Ben Williams, Dog Trainer

CHAPTER 12

The Last Bark

Bathrobe cinched, I called for Maui as I walked through the house on the way to our meditation room. She raced past me and stood by the chair. Once I sat, she jumped onto my lap.

"We've got this down pretty good, don't we Maui?"

She wagged her tail.

We've been meditating together for enough years that we've experienced first hand its transformative benefits. You and your dog can, too.

I hope, throughout this book, that I've taken the mystique out of the process of meditation — without losing meditation's inherent mystery.

The benefits I've discussed can happen to anyone willing to put forth the effort to meditate, but there are more, many more.

Part of the mystery is that our meditation experiences, as well as the additional benefits that we might reap, are as individual as our dogs.

I looked at Maui. I could tell from the gleam in her eye that she remembered the early days, when getting ourselves ready to meditate was more of a challenge.

It was fun — don't get me wrong. I loved every minute of it.

But to save forests, I edited out many of the scenarios we experienced on our meditation journey.

It was an adventure, though. Meditation always is.

And it's a story to be shared.

We shared ours with you, and we invite you to share yours with us at www.DogMeditation.com.

Now, out of great fondness and respect for my guru, I'll give Maui the last word.

 *Aaaaarfff*

Appendices

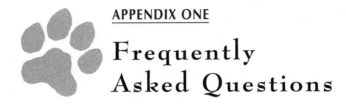

Frequently Asked Questions

Is there a specific length of time I should meditate?

Many traditions specify twenty or thirty minutes, or even more, once or twice a day. But any meditation is better than none. Start with a short time, like five minutes, and expand the time if you can. Twenty to thirty minutes a day is a good length to aim for, but ten minutes is great, too.

How important is regular meditation practice?

Regular meditation is like regular exercise. You may be able to get a runner's high during your first run, but you won't get the full physiological benefits unless you make running, or other exercise, a regular part of your schedule.

Should I keep my eyes closed or open?

This is entirely up to each individual and depends on the type of meditation. If you tend to fall asleep or get drowsy with your eyes shut, it might be wise to meditate with your eyes open, but with your gaze softened and relaxed. You can gaze at something meaningful, like a statue or a picture of a spiritual teacher, or at a spot three or four feet in front of you on the floor.

If you use a candle, flower, or other visual object as part of your ritual, then keep your eyes at least partly open. Of course, if you are doing an active meditation such as walking or chopping vegetables, then keep your eyes wide open.

What if I experience physical pain when I meditate?

Sensations like itching, aches, or other discomforts can occur during meditation. To minimize them, you want to be sure to sit comfortably with good posture. If you still have aches and pains, it might be because your mind is quieter and you notice what you normally ignore. Sometimes, when you quiet the mind, your body becomes "noisy" to try to distract you from meditation.

But a quiet body contributes to a quiet mind. If you sit through the discomfort, and breathe into it, oftentimes the discomfort will diminish in a few minutes. If not, or if you experience pain rather than discomfort, then move to get comfortable. Life is hard enough without making meditation a test of endurance.

How can I learn to meditate from a book?

You can read about meditation from a book, but you can learn it by putting the suggestions into practice. Simply, you learn by doing.

What do I do if I get drowsy or fall asleep while I meditate?

First, meditate at a time when you are fully awake, preferably not soon after eating. Second, if you meditate first thing in the morning you might want to wash your face or drink some water beforehand. If that doesn't work, try meditating with your eyes open, or turning on a soft light if the room is dark. You can meditate outside, or near an open window to get fresh air, or try walking meditation. You can also put on music, or try Sacred Verse Meditation, or

Conscious Activity Meditation. Be creative, be patient, and have fun.

Is meditation self-hypnosis?

No. Self-hypnosis and meditation are both restful, but they are entirely different states of consciousness. Self-hypnosis and meditation both begin by focusing attention. But in meditation, you stay conscious and centered in the present moment. Self-hypnosis requires a specific semi-conscious state in which you are open to a particular, pre-established suggestion.

Do I have to "believe" in meditation for it to work?

No. A little skepticism is healthy. But down-right hostility probably won't get you very far. It serves you best to suspend disbelief as you try meditation and experience the benefits for yourself.

Does meditation have any ethical implications?

If anything, meditation tends to help people become more ethical, and more committed to the individual ethics that they hold. You may even find your ethical horizons broaden. Many times meditation strengthens the connection you feel to others and to the world. This increased awareness may influence your values, almost exclusively for the good.

Does meditation have any religious implications or affiliations?

Many faiths, including Christianity, Judaism, Islam, Buddhism, and Hinduism have meditation traditions. Meditation itself is non-dogmatic; it doesn't even require a belief in a higher being. You can bring religion to meditation by infusing rituals with religious significance. Or you can simply sit quietly and breathe. The benefits are the same.

Remember this simple wisdom: The essence of meditation is the non-judgmental observation of the present moment.

With a river that wide, the possibilities of exploring it seem endless.

Active Compassion

Challenging dogs can be the joy or the bane of our lives. Some dogs are a challenge because they have been abused, neglected or abandoned. Some just seem to be born that way. No matter what their history, though, challenging dogs take more time and energy than other dogs.

They can make us crazy, but they can also stretch our hearts and souls.

In any case, caring for a challenging dog calls for active compassion, or tough love.

It's not as daunting as it may sound. In fact, compassion in action is a profound spiritual practice, and meditation, with or without a dog, can help us cultivate greater compassion.

Because each dog is a challenge in its own way, it's difficult to address the myriad of issues that a dog lover might encounter.

An article on www.DogMeditation.com explains Active Compassion in depth. In addition, I've listed resources that can help dog lovers find positive, practical ways to address the unique challenges posed by individual dogs.

Glossary

The following are definitions based on how the words are used in this text, not general definitions.

Alpha: Leader; chief dog.

Alter/Alteration: The process of changing a negative statement or thought to an empowering one.

Awareness: The quality of being conscious of and attentive to thoughts, emotions, and motivations.

Belief: The practice of knowing something to be possible.

Bliss: The contentment and peace we find when our mind is still, as it is in the moments we are in the gap.

Compassion: The art of being gentle and loving, of embracing objectivity, invoking patience and exercising forgiveness.

The Cycle: The process of observing a thought, letting it go, and returning to a focal point.

The Gap: The space between thoughts.

Guru: A spiritual teacher, or an expert in a certain, usually spiritual, field.

Hound-lounge: The state between full awareness and sleep that a dog stays in much of the time.

Intention: The willful purpose or conscious choice that we bring to an action or state.

Intuition: The human version of instinct, often called the "little voice."

Negative Puppy Mind: Negative, destructive, or unwanted thoughts that invade the mind.

Objectivity: The practice of stepping out of the immediacy of a situation or emotion and looking at it impartially.

The Observer: A detached part of ourselves that witnesses our thoughts.

Puppy Mind: The mind as it jumps randomly from one thought to the next. A busy or restless mind.

Ritual: The process of using external gestures or symbols to induce an internal state. Ritual is also a strategy we can use to signal our bodies and minds that it's time to meditate.

Spontaneous Meditation: The times that we "zone out" without conscious effort and are in the space between thoughts.

Synch: The harmonization or synchronization of our breath with our dogs' breathing pattern.

Synergy: In meditation, synergy is the law of "where two or more are gathered," meaning that when two or more beings are united in intention and belief, their efforts are exponentially more powerful than their individual efforts.

FREE
Meditation CD

In an effort to make meditation as easy as possible, I've compiled a CD that can be used during meditation, either with or without a dog.

One track is ten minutes long and guides the listener into and out of a brief meditation, with soft music in the background. This track is useful when first starting to meditate, so that you can relax and follow the cues to ease into and out of meditation until you get the hang of it.

The next track is twenty minutes. It guides the listener through a longer meditation, with fewer cues than the first track. In the background is specially composed music to help facilitate a meditative state. This track is most useful when you don't need as many cues, or when you want a twenty-minute meditation without having to keep track of time.

The last track is twenty minutes of meditation music with no speaking at all.

The CD is free if you download it from www.DogMeditation.com and use the code: dog3452 at the appropriate prompt.

If you don't want to download, you can receive your free CD by mail, for a small shipping and handling charge of $4.95. Just register at www.DogMeditation.com or complete the order form at the back of the book.

From Fido to Feline

$16.97 Hardcover
ISBN: 0975263129

The "tail" continues with *How to Meditate with Your Cat: An Introduction to Meditation for Cat Lovers*. James Jacobson shows how to turn quiet moments with a cat into the heart of a purrrfect meditation practice.

Order Form

The quickest, most secure way to order is via our web site at www.DogMeditation.com. If you prefer to use a check or money order, please fill out the form and mail to:

Maui Media P.O. Box 1200 Puunene, HI 96784-1200

Title	Price	Qty.	Subtotal
Dog Meditation CD (limited to 1 per household)	FREE		
How to Meditate with Your Dog hardcover book	$16.95		
How to Meditate with Your Dog audio book on CD	$19.95		
How to Meditate with Your Cat hardcover book	$16.95		
How to Meditate with Your Cat audio book on CD	$19.95		
Shipping & Handling: U.S.: $4.95 for the first item, $ 2.00 for each additional product. International: Please see www.DogMeditation.com to order.			
Sales Tax: Please add 4.167% tax for items shipped to Hawaii addresses			
Total (in US dollars):			

Name: _____

Address: _____

City: _____ State: _____ Zip Code: _____

Telephone: (if we have questions about your order) _____

Email Address: _____

Payment: ☐ Check   ☐ Money Orders   ☐ Credit Card
           ☐ Visa   ☐ Master Card   ☐ Discover   ☐ Amex

Credit Card Number: _____

Expiration Date: _____ Signature: _____

For credit card orders, you may fax this form to 808-442-1180.
Telephone Orders: Call 888-778-1685